Headline Series

No. 283   FOREIGN POLICY ASSOCIATION $4.00

GLOBAL TELEVISION AND FOREIGN POLICY

by James F. Larson

	Introduction by Edwin Newman	3
1	Television's Role in U.S. Foreign Policy...	5
2	Technology, Economics and the Public ..	15
3	Window on the World...............................	29
4	Television 'Diplomacy'	43
5	Public Influence on Foreign Policy	52
6	Reform or Radical Redefinition?..............	63
	Talking It Over...	70
	Reading List	71

Cover Design: Ed Bohon

Mar./Apr. 1987
Published February 1988

LAMAR UNIVERSITY LIBRARY

The Author

JAMES F. LARSON is on the faculty of the School of Communications, University of Washington, Seattle. During 1985–86 he was a Fulbright Scholar in the Department of Mass Communication, Yonsei University, Seoul, South Korea. He holds a doctorate in communication from Stanford University. Professor Larson is the author of *Television's Window on the World: International Affairs Coverage on the U.S. Networks* (Norwood, N.J., Ablex Publishing Corp., 1984). His primary research and teaching activities are in international communication, combined with a special interest in Asia.

The Foreign Policy Association

The Foreign Policy Association is a private, nonprofit, nonpartisan educational organization. Its purpose is to stimulate wider interest and more effective participation in, and greater understanding of, world affairs among American citizens. Among its activities is the continuous publication, dating from 1935, of the HEADLINE SERIES. The author is responsible for factual accuracy and for the views expressed. FPA itself takes no position on issues of U.S. foreign policy.

HEADLINE SERIES (ISSN 0017-8780) is published five times a year, January, March, May, September and November, by the Foreign Policy Association, Inc., 729 Seventh Ave., New York, N.Y. 10019. Chairman, Robert V. Lindsay; President, John W. Kiermaier; Editor in Chief, Nancy L. Hoepli; Senior Editor, Ann R. Monjo; Associate Editor, K. M. Rohan. Subscription rates, $15.00 for 5 issues; $25.00 for 10 issues; $30.00 for 15 issues. Single copy price $4.00. Discount 25% on 10 to 99 copies; 30% on 100 to 499; 35% on 500 to 999; 40% on 1,000 or more. Payment must accompany order for $8 or less. Add $1 for postage. Second-class postage paid at New York, N.Y. POSTMASTER: Send address changes to HEADLINE SERIES, Foreign Policy Association, 729 Seventh Ave., New York, N.Y. 10019. Copyright 1988 by Foreign Policy Association, Inc. Composed and printed at Science Press, Ephrata, Pennsylvania.

Library of Congress Catalog Card No. 87-72369
ISBN 0-87124-117-X

Introduction

Professor Larson's study could not be more timely. While he was finishing it, a helicopter on charter to CBS News in the Persian Gulf rescued 29 crew members of a Cypriot tanker loaded with Saudi Arabian oil and set afire during an attack by an Iranian gunboat. Here, indeed, newspeople were not merely observers but participants, shaping events as well as reporting them.

The rescue, to be sure, was a happy accident (though it should be borne in mind that, by definition, the news business often deals in what happens by accident, by chance). Yet even if we leave the Persian Gulf incident aside, Professor Larson's study could not come at a more opportune time. The importance of television has seldom, if ever, been more graphically demonstrated than it was during the December 1987 Reagan-Gorbachev meeting in Washington. It was possible to get the impression that General Secretary Gorbachev went to Washington less to see the President than to get on American television whenever he—and other members of his delegation, as well—could. Mr. Gorbachev's hour-and-a-quarter opening statement at his so-called news conference just before he left for East Berlin and then home was a telling example of how television may be exploited and of the decisions people in television sometimes must make. As Mr. Gorbachev rambled past the one-hour mark, ABC, CBS and NBC decided to pull away. Their evening news programs were coming up. They wanted to present their versions of the story, naturally including references to what Mr. Gorbachev had to say. CNN, on the other hand, stayed with him to the end. Yet another Gorbachev extravaganza is promised in Moscow in 1988.

We hear a great deal about news management and how governments may manipulate television. As Mr. Gorbachev was the latest to show, they do manipulate it. When they do, however, they are recognizing its power, capitalizing on that power, and at the same time enhancing it. Indeed, it may be argued that they have no choice. In the making of foreign policy in countries where some public understanding and support is thought to be necessary or desirable, television is one of the principal factors policymakers must take into account. They know that television will have much to do with the way their policy is judged, and with public impressions of what its chance of success may be.

Professor Larson sheds valuable light on these matters, and on many more, including the startling technological changes that have already taken place and the even more startling changes still to come. He tells us about the significance of the manner in which television presents news, quite different from that of the press, because it gets away from the familiar print pattern of the "lead" followed by details, and instead arranges fact and interpretation in what is intended to be a coherent, and if possible dramatic, whole. He cites the extent to which those in charge of foreign policy depend on television for information and how, sometimes, they use it to float ideas and for not quite formal negotiation.

There is much more: the possible consequences of the recent cuts in network news departments; the biases of television news, that is, the stories and countries it habitually covers and those it does not; the way television may influence foreign policy through reporting that creates an impression, favorable or unfavorable, of the country to which that policy may apply; the degree to which television journalists may become part of the policy process through the questions they ask. These questions may well define the limits of public discussion.

The impact of television on foreign policy, an impact Professor Larson believes represents "a quantum leap" over the historic role of the press, is a slippery subject. Generalization is easy, nailing things down quite the opposite. Even organizing the subject and raising the pertinent questions is difficult. Professor Larson has organized the subject and raised the pertinent questions with a clarity that will be notably helpful to members of the foreign policy establishment, to people in the news business itself, and—which counts most—to the public.

Edwin Newman,
December 1987   *TV news commentator and author*

1

Television's Role in U.S. Foreign Policy

The rapid evolution of television news since the early 1970s coincides with fundamental changes in the conduct of foreign policy and international diplomacy. In the words of the Israeli statesman and diplomat Abba Eban, "Any discussion of changes in the diplomatic system must begin with the most potent and far-reaching transformation of all: the collapse of reticence and privacy in negotiation. The intrusion of the media into every phase and level of the negotiation process changes the whole spirit and nature of diplomacy."

The contemporary changes in media and foreign policy are transnational—that is, they extend beyond national boundaries—and hold significance for virtually all nations in the world. However, they are especially pronounced in the United States, with its global involvement in international affairs, its competitive, commercially supported media system, and a national political environment in which television is ever more prominent. Furthermore, the United States deserves special scrutiny because of its dominant role in the international media system. That dominance itself surfaced as a foreign policy issue in the 1970s with international discussion, particularly among the nations of the Third World, of the call for a New International Information Order.

While there is a consensus that both television and foreign policy have changed dramatically, there is little agreement about the ways in which the change has affected the structural relationship between them. Lloyd N. Cutler, who served as White House counsel for President Jimmy Carter during the Iran hostage crisis, claims that "TV news now has a much greater effect on national policy decisions—especially foreign policy decisions— than print journalism has ever been able to achieve and more than most experienced observers realize." By contrast, many political scientists contend that, on matters of foreign policy, television is subject to government news management and conveys elite views of America's overseas interests in all but exceptional circumstances. From such a perspective, television coverage and its potential impact on public opinion are factors to be planned and controlled in the implementation of foreign policy. The purpose of this HEADLINE SERIES is to explore such competing views and the complexities of a changing media-foreign policy relationship in an era of global television.

In 1987, as this is written, the Iran-contra arms scandal is but the latest international affair symptomatic of the more profound, long-term changes television brings to the media-foreign policy relationship. Ironically, it involves the Administration of President Ronald Reagan, a former movie actor frequently referred to as the great communicator because of his skillful use of television. The involvement of Iran is perhaps the most profound irony in the whole affair.

In November 1979 the U.S. embassy in Tehran was taken over and Americans were held hostage for 444 days. That protracted hostage crisis is widely viewed as a watershed event in the evolving relationship of media and foreign policy. It focused public debate on practices of the major television news organizations and their interaction with government officials here and in other nations, and many have speculated that it was the single

Auth © 1985 *The Philadelphia Inquirer.*
Reprinted with permission of Universal Press Syndicate. All rights reserved.

major factor in the defeat of Carter in the 1980 presidential election.

The release of the hostages on the day of President Reagan's inauguration provided a unique and historic confluence of foreign policy and television coverage. The U.S. television networks drew on all their resources for global newsgathering in order to cover simultaneously the two events half a world apart.

President Reagan neared the end of his presidency under the cloud of a major foreign policy failure that in some ways brought the hostage affair full circle. Like the earlier crisis, it involved Iran, it concerned American hostages in the Middle East and it elicited persistent television news attention. When news of the covert action in the Iran-contra affair became public, it did so instantly, visually, and with the large global reach of television. Because the affair involved U.S. policy toward Iran, Israel, Nicaragua, Iraq and Lebanon and because numerous other nations also had a stake in the matter, particularly U.S. allies in the Middle East and Europe, it provided a showcase for the new capabilities of satellite television. In 1986 and 1987 such programs as *ABC News Nightline* and the *MacNeil/Lehrer Newshour* on the Public Broadcasting Service (PBS) brought together in live conversations government officials and policy elites from many of the nations involved.

From a television standpoint, the Iran-contra affair was also tailor-made to exploit the heavy presence maintained by commercial and public television organizations in Washington, D.C. The televised joint hearings by the select committees of the Senate and House of Representatives during the summer of 1987 received massive attention in the United States and considerable coverage in other nations. Lieutenant Colonel Oliver North, the National Security Council staff member centrally involved in covert activities, became an overnight celebrity during his televised testimony. Opinion polls taken at the time showed a sharp jump in public support for the Nicaraguan contras. In contrast with other witnesses who appeared before the congressional committees, North provided a dazzling display of television's emotive power and its ability to convey appearance or image as opposed to the more abstract thought and substance of testimony.

From a policy perspective, the Iran-contra hearings represented an effort by Congress to rally public support in the perennial struggle over congressional versus presidential influence in foreign policy. In all likelihood, this issue of influence and control over foreign policy was the major reason for televising the hearings. By doing so, Congress was able to reach a broad segment of the public through a medium more characteristically dominated by the President and members of the executive branch of government.

Although extensive in its consequences for U.S. foreign policy and illustrative of underlying changes in the media-foreign policy relationship, the Iran-contra affair is only one in a long series of events marking the evolution of global television news. Indeed, one effect of television is to lend a more profoundly visual cast to collective memory and to history itself. Both the present and past decades are punctuated by events that were visually recorded and often widely broadcast by television. Too numerous to catalogue, they include such occurrences as President Richard M. Nixon's

1972 visit to China, the final years of the Vietnam War, Egyptian President Anwar al-Sadat's visit to Jerusalem in 1977, his assassination in 1981, the Ethiopian famine in 1984, the hijacking of TWA Flight 847 by Lebanese Shiites in 1985, and the victory of Corazon C. Aquino and "people power" in the Philippines during 1986.

Occurrences that receive no television coverage may be as significant as those crises or episodes of television diplomacy that draw saturation coverage. Events like the brutal killings in Cambodia from 1975 through 1979 or the Indonesian invasion of East Timor in 1978, and the mass murder which ensued, were scarcely noticed by U.S. television news.

Such blind spots in television news coverage occur not only in certain nations or in regard to particular events but also reflect broader, long-term patterns of coverage. For example, consistently high levels of attention to nations in Western Europe and consistently low levels of attention to those of sub-Saharan Africa may reveal as much about the relationship of television to foreign policy as does coverage of particular countries or occurrences at a particular point in time. The same general observation about patterns of coverage and their relationship to foreign policy applies to the print media as well.

Rethinking the Media-Foreign Policy Relationship

The concurrent rapid changes in both television and foreign policy require a reformulation of traditional thought about the overall relationship between the media and foreign policy for several reasons. First, most scholarly literature on the subject was written before satellite, video, electronic and transportation technologies brought televised international news to its present state. Today, circumstances increasingly undermine the 1960s conventional wisdom that the elite printed press is more important than television as a factor in foreign policy.

Second, political scientists have characteristically thought of foreign policy as an area apart from domestic social forces, with the mass media, elections and organized interest groups acting as intervening variables between "domestic" and "foreign" phenomena. Implicit in this view is that foreign events take place in distant locations while domestic events are close to home. The international character of communication industries blurs that distinction. Also, satellite television appears to compress the perceived distances among nations or their policy elites, making the traditional conceptual approach more difficult to apply.

Third, a rather widespread traditional view holds that the media and policymakers find themselves in an adversarial relationship or one that is, at best, an uneasy symbiosis. However, contemporary institutions responsible for broadcast television on the one hand and foreign policy on the other often work so closely together that their roles appear to merge. When they do, it may be most appropriate to think of them as a single institution.

This HEADLINE SERIES will extend a conception of the media-foreign policy relationship suggested by political scientist Bernard C. Cohen in *The Press and Foreign Policy* (Princeton University Press, 1963). Before doing so, it is necessary to explain and clarify the terms "foreign policy" and "diplomacy" as used here and to stress the need for a modicum of historical perspective.

In the following pages, foreign policy will generally refer to a process of planning and implementation: choosing goals in the conduct of one nation's relations with others and selecting strategies and tactics for achieving those goals. Diplomacy, on the other hand, is fundamentally a communication process: it is the art or practice of communicating the substance of one government's policies to other governments. As such, diplomacy is part of the implementation rather than the planning phase of foreign policy.

As early as 1941 Harold Lasswell, a pioneering communication researcher, stressed the importance of seeing the communication process as a series of attention frames in which the stream of public attention is related to policy. His "World Attention Survey" was explicitly global in focus, analyzing references to symbols of nations in the press of other nations. Such symbols included references to the names of leaders, nations, policies or institutions. For example, a headline such as "British Respect German Airmen" in a U.S. newspaper would contain significant

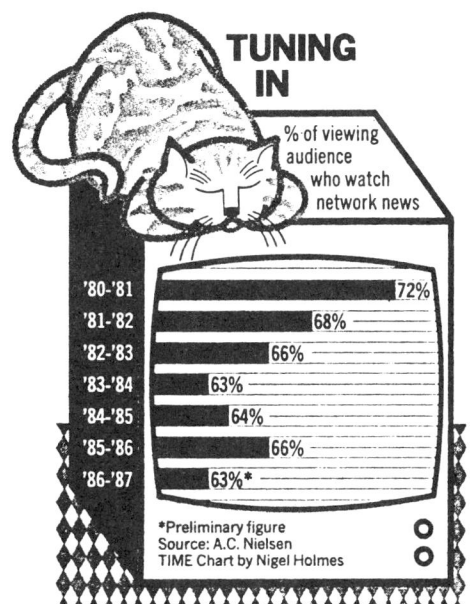

Copyright 1987 Time Inc. All rights reserved.
Reprinted by permission from TIME.

symbols referring to both Britain and Germany. His working assumption was that people and nations cannot respond to an environment that is not brought to their notice. Hence, the need to describe fluctuations of collective attention in order to examine and understand policy. Although produced much earlier, the logic of Lasswell's work applies in the present era of global television.

Even within the relatively short history of television itself, some of the research and thought on the nature of that medium and its political impact provide a start toward assessing its more global role in relation to foreign policy. In 1951, during the early days of television news, Kurt and Gladys Engel Lang compared live public observation of an event with the video image of that same event broadcast by television. The occasion was a large Chicago parade welcoming General Douglas MacArthur home after President Harry S. Truman had relieved him of command in Korea. The Langs stationed numerous observers along the parade route in order to compare their reports with an audio tape and detailed written descriptions of the television coverage. Furthermore, they did so not in an era of lightweight, hand-held Minicams, but rather in one of bulky, heavy television cameras, newsfilm and audio tape. Their findings showed that most of the onlookers at the parade expected to see a wild spectacle, based in large part on prior media coverage of MacArthur's return to the United States. Only a few attended the parade because of active hero worship. Many were disappointed, commenting that "We should have stayed home and watched it on TV." While spectators were fortunate to catch a brief glimpse of the general and his family, television coverage made him the almost continuous center of attention. Use of closeup shots and accompanying commentary helped to personalize the event for the television viewer.

The Langs succeeded in an early and important demonstration of three aspects of television. First, it conveys an "unwitting bias" due to the very nature of television technology. In other words, the television image is inherently a refracted image. Second, it provides a unified and personalized picture of events, through the structuring of visuals and commentary. Third, television coverage itself can modify events by encouraging staging to make them more suitable for broadcast and by creating consciousness among participants in the event of a wider television audience. In 1980, CBS News correspondent Bert Quint, who covered the Iran hostage crisis, described coverage of demonstrators outside the American embassy in Tehran who shouted "Death to the shah," "Death to Carter," and "Death to America." As he put it, ". . . whenever you pointed a camera anywhere in the direction of these crowds, the chorus would break into its theme song." Much of the demonstrating was for the benefit of U.S. television cameras.

TV and the Foreign Policy Process

What does current experience with television confirm about the relationship of the news media to foreign policy and what does television accentuate, diminish or otherwise change in that relationship? To treat these important questions, the following pages focus on global television and foreign policy not in isolation but in relation to other news media and in the broad context in which U.S. foreign policy is debated, designed and implemented.

In the early 1960s Bernard Cohen noted that, in general, the media act as observer, participant and catalyst in foreign policy. These roles are not exclusive of one another, but they appear to be comprehensive. It is difficult to conceive of any activity of the media, including television, that cannot be described in terms of one or more of these broad categories.

Television's role as an **observer** of foreign policy is significantly influenced by
- its relationship to other major media, such as wire services and newspapers;
- the background, training and practices of correspondents, camera personnel, producers and editors;
- those organizational and economic factors that most strongly influence the gathering and dissemination of television news;
- changes brought about by the introduction of new technology for observing international affairs;
- international and transnational concerns that impinge directly upon the activities of U.S. television news organizations; and
- the nature of international affairs content, which is constantly, if gradually, changing.

The **participant** role of television, as with other media, can be thought of as an interaction or symbiotic relationship between television and policymaker. Policymakers make regular contributions to television coverage through formal press conferences, briefings, background papers and leaks. Television, along with the print media, contributes on a regular and timely basis to official knowledge of policy-related developments in international affairs.

Television serves as a **catalyst** for change in foreign policy by influencing public opinion. Current studies of public opinion show that there are sharp gradations of interest in international affairs. Those with the greatest interest in foreign policy are small in number—policy officials and influential elites. The largest portion of the population has relatively little interest in foreign policy and international affairs except in extraordinary circumstances.

In general, it is through the elites and the attentive public that television and other media contribute to changes in American foreign policy. Television's effect on official perceptions of public opinion is more important than the actual opinions of the large, inattentive segment of the public. In other words, if officials responsible for policy believe that public opinion weighs strongly in one direction or another, they may act on those beliefs, regardless of the actual nature and depth of the public opinion. Alternatively, elected officials and policy elites may pay more attention to the public dialogue among their peers in the belief that it has a predictable relationship to broad public opinion, either shaping or reflecting it. From such a perspective, the limited-effects view of the mass media adopted by many social scientists, based on voluminous research during the 1960s and early 1970s into the effects of televised violence, is only marginally relevant. The key questions concerning television's capacity to change foreign policy revolve around its influence on the perceptions and actions of those who make or most directly affect that policy.

Cohen's conception of the media's roles poses several problems. It was developed as an approach to thinking about the foreign policy of one nation, the United States, and as such may obscure important international considerations. It does not call attention to questions about how the timing of television news broadcasts, as distinct from print media, may relate to timing in the foreign policy process. And it may encourage a similar lack of attention to perceptions of spatial relationships by policymakers, media and the public. It views the media (here television) and foreign policy as a relationship between two separate processes and institutions when, in many instances, the two might better be seen as one.

2

Technology, Economics and the Public

The rise of television news to its dominant position as an influence on the politics of foreign policy can be traced to technology, economics, public reliance on television as a news source and a set of international concerns. All help to explain the new circumstances facing policymakers, the press and the public.

Of the principal technologies that exert a strong, synergistic effect on television and foreign policy, the **communication satellite** is undoubtedly the most conspicuous. U.S. television audiences became familiar with satellite transmission and the on-screen graphic "Live Via Satellite" in the 1960s, when the commercial networks used satellites such as Telstar and Early Bird. In 1972, only 43 nations possessed Intelsat earth stations or terrestrial links to that system, which was the major channel for satellite transmission of television pictures. By the mid-1980s, Intelsat had 109 member states and provided communication links among some 170 nations and territories.

Today, the U.S. television networks take portable equipment called "flyaways" with them to foreign or domestic areas where satellite uplink facilities are not available or convenient. Such equipment is small enough to be transported aboard a Lear jet or checked as baggage on a passenger plane. In early 1986, CBS and NBC used such portable uplinks in Manila during their coverage of the Philippine election that brought President Aquino to power.

During the Reagan Administration, the U.S. government has greatly increased its own capability for use of satellite television through expansion of the Worldnet program administered by the United States Information Agency. This program provides another channel through which the government can convey official views and other televised information to many nations.

Currently, several innovative projects are under way that may well be harbingers of television and its role in foreign policy in the 21st century. In the spring of 1987, New York- and London-based corporations announced an intent to create Planet 3, the first global television news program. The idea was to use multinational television linkages via satellite to compare the way particular news events are covered in different parts of the world. Video segments would be accompanied by narration in the language of each country in which the broadcasts are shown. Later in 1987, the Cable News Network (CNN) announced plans for a global newscast entitled *CNN World Report*. Based on the same principle as Planet 3, the six-hour program each Sunday would invite all nations recognized by the United Nations to participate. The goal of the program is to invite each nation to report on events and issues deemed important, with translation provided for recipient nations.

Another key technology is **electronic newsgathering**, the portable, lightweight cameras and editing equipment used in television news. As this hardware becomes smaller, incorporates more-powerful editing capabilities, and eventually allows transmission directly from television correspondent to satellite, it promises to make governmental restriction on the gathering and dissemination of visual news much more difficult.

A third technology is **modern air travel**, which has changed both diplomacy and its coverage by television. The prospect of newer travel technologies, such as hypersonic suborbital vehicles, suggests a future continuation of such influence.

A fourth technology, **computers and microelectronics**, is perhaps most pervasive of all, being integrated with each of the preceding. Broadcast newsrooms have been computerized, and systems such as Newstar at CBS News have the capacity for searching through computerized film, tape and newspaper clipping archives, storing and calling up stories from all major wire services, and keeping track of stories and camera crews. Producers or reporters from CBS bureaus around the world can tap into the Newstar system with IBM personal computers. For example, a reporter in the Tokyo bureau can transmit a script to New York or Washington and also check on what is available in the CBS film and tape archives. The system will also interface with the small, notebook-size word-processing computers that are becoming popular with television journalists. Teleprompters, which display and scroll magnified versions of a script for correspondents to read on the air, are also part of the system.

One of the most interesting and potentially far-reaching technologies that can have an impact on television and foreign policy is the **remote-sensing satellite**. The Chernobyl disaster, in which fallout from the massive amounts of radiation released by the Soviet nuclear plant reached many European nations and the United States, provides the best illustration to date of how remote-sensing satellite technology can influence government policy. In this case the Soviet Union attempted to suppress release of information about the accident to the news media, and it was U.S. and other Western television organizations that broadcast photographs of the damaged reactor taken by the U.S. Landsat and the French SPOT remote-sensing satellites. Within the next decade, it is possible that news organizations will be able to take pictures from advanced remote-sensing satellites of any place on earth, producing highly detailed images, according to a recent *Issues in Science and Technology*.

A May 1987 memorandum produced by the Congressional Office of Technology Assessment included the following key findings:

- While it is possible to build a "mediasat" system with high resolution, timely global coverage and assured access to data using current technology, the cost of such a system might well exceed revenues.
- A mediasat would probably compound problems inherent in the management of national security and foreign policy in a spirited democracy, but such problems would likely be manageable.
- Within a decade, many nations will have their own remote-sensing systems. It is unclear whether the U.S. government could effectively limit or control media access to satellite imagery if foreign governments do not exercise similar controls.

As changes in law, technology and the marketplace make remote sensing a worldwide private industry, the use of satellite images by news organizations will raise such issues as First Amendment rights, national security concerns, international treaty obligations and relations between sovereign states. The foreign policy and national security questions include media coverage of military operations, possible retaliation by foreign governments for media disclosures, loss of government control during a crisis because of nearly instantaneous media disclosures, the provision of valuable intelligence data to third parties, and possible media misinterpretation of satellite data.

The U.S. government response to such foreign policy concerns was reflected in an August 1987 Commerce Department rule that gives the secretaries of State and Defense the power to veto license applications or suspend operations of U.S. commercial remote-sensing satellite organizations on national security or foreign policy grounds. Under the rule, which would not apply to the SPOT Image Corporation, the organization which markets data from the French SPOT satellite, license applications will be sent to the Defense and State departments for review.

Smaller technologies also impinge on the media-foreign policy relationship. Audiocassette recordings of Ayatollah Ruhollah Khomeini and other religious leaders played a well-documented role in the revolution which overthrew the shah in Iran. Many of these recordings were made in France and smuggled into Iran before Khomeini's return. In the Republic of Korea, accounts of the bloody 1980 Kwangju incident, videotaped by Japanese, West German and U.S. news organizations, circulated widely among university students and other opposition groups during ensuing years. Along with photographs and written accounts, they undeniably strengthened opposition to the government of President Chun Doo Hwan.

Economics

Economic changes have accompanied the evolution of technology. As business enterprises, the U.S. television networks are engaged in selling audiences to advertisers. The income of network news organizations is determined by the total size of the audience they attract and maintain for their broadcasts. For a period of time during the late 1970s the news divisions of the ABC, CBS and NBC television networks all earned net profits, something they had not generally been expected to do in earlier years. More recently they have fallen on harder times and lower audience share due partly to competition from cable television and the proliferation of such new technologies as the videocassette recorder. Current estimates show the combined budgets of the three national networks exceed their combined revenues. Several factors helped to explain the changing economic picture for network television news.

One was that local affiliate stations of the national networks recognized the profitability of news. Efforts to expand the flagship network broadcasts to a full hour, including one as late as 1981, were defeated by affiliates who were reluctant to give up valuable advertising time and chose instead to lengthen their own news broadcasts.

Even as the advertising revenue from television news increased, the costs for satellite transmission of visual news from many points around the globe to the United States decreased dramatically. For television news organizations in this country, the cost of satellite time—once decisive—has become less and less a factor in coverage of international affairs.

One consequence of the technological and economic changes

strongly evident by the early 1980s was the increased coverage that local television stations gave international events, particularly those with a strong "local angle." A local television station in Kansas City, Missouri, for example, dispatched a crew to cover U.S. officials who were monitoring the presidential election in El Salvador during the spring of 1984. The head of the observer delegation was Senator Nancy L. Kassebaum (R-Kans.). In another case, when hundreds of people died in a natural gas explosion in Mexico City in November 1984, a Los Angeles station, whose viewing audience was 26 percent Hispanic, sent a crew to provide live coverage.

Visnews International, a principal supplier of video footage for television organizations around the world, now offers a service to local stations which includes camera crews, production facilities and other resources. The service is small but growing.

In addition to competition from local affiliates, the networks responded to competition among themselves by maintaining a costly infrastructure of bureaus and highly paid correspondents. According to *Broadcasting* magazine, the typical network of the mid-1980s had 23 bureaus, 15 of them overseas. It also employed approximately 100 correspondents earning an average of $150,000 each. The total cost of maintaining a bureau ranged from $500,000 to more than $2 million. Salaries and travel accounted for about three quarters of the cost of a foreign bureau.

In the face of such costs, a major problem for ABC, CBS and NBC is their lack of enough time slots to use much of the material generated by their news divisions. One solution to that problem is to amortize the news division costs over a 24-hour schedule, as done by CNN. Another alternative is greater cooperation and less duplication of effort among the networks in gathering visual news from abroad. Don Hewitt, executive producer of CBS's *60 Minutes*, recently suggested that the networks jointly create a visual "wire service" for television to replace the present structure in which all three networks maintain costly bureaus in many of the same cities overseas.

At stake for the three major commercial news organizations are the future relationships between local affiliates and the national networks and perhaps even the long-term viability of network news. Local affiliates now frequently air the half-hour network news broadcasts of CBS, NBC and ABC following two hours of their own news. One network study concluded that in 1985 the average person watched almost twice as much local news as network news—76 minutes per week of network news and 146 minutes of local news. In the 1980-81 season, 72 percent of American households watching television were tuned to the three network news shows. In 1986 that figure dropped to about 66 percent, and in early 1987 it was down to 62 percent nationally. However, in Chicago—an example of particular concern to the networks—just 51 percent of viewers were watching network news. Network executives concerned with keeping that audience from tuning them out recognize that they must provide something different. Here the commercial news organizations face a dilemma. On the one hand, executives publicly claim that in the future they will differentiate themselves from local stations by providing more and better world news. On the other, they decry the increasing costs of covering international affairs, despite the reduced cost of satellite time.

During the latest round of severe cutbacks at CBS News in March 1987, 215 people (including 14 on-air reporters) were dismissed, and overseas bureaus in Warsaw and Bangkok were closed. The cuts moved *CBS Evening News* anchor Dan Rather to write as follows in *The New York Times*. "We have lost correspondents, producers, camera crews. That means we will cover less news. We will go to fewer places and witness fewer events....Our concern, beyond the shattered lives of valued friends and colleagues is, How do we go on? How do we cover the world?"

Television: Main Source of International News

For many years the three major commercial networks have used a coordinated promotional approach to convince the public that they are the leading sources of international, as distinct from national, regional or local, news. All three networks integrate images of the globe or world maps into their New York anchor location sets. ABC News is "Uniquely Qualified to Bring You the World," and elements of the marketing communications of the other two networks make the same point, if in different words.

There is a sound strategic basis for promoting network news as superior in the quality of its international affairs coverage. As noted above, the commercial networks are large international organizations with news budgets enabling them to cover significant world events. Of even greater consequence, the American public views network television as more international in character than competing news media.

Beginning in the late 1960s or early 1970s, television replaced newspapers as the public's preferred source of news and public affairs information. The shift in preference is documented by both television and newspaper industry-sponsored surveys. The most frequently cited surveys are the Roper polls conducted every few years since 1959 for the Television Information Office. The initial question in each Roper survey has remained the same over the years: "First, I'd like to ask you where you usually get most of your news about what's going on in the world today—from the newspapers or radio or television or magazines or talking to people or where?" (Multiple responses were permitted.) In 1959 only 51 percent of respondents cited television, compared with an average of 65 percent of respondents in the seven polls taken since 1972. Fifty-seven percent cited newspapers in the 1959 survey, but that decreased to an average of 46 percent of respondents in the seven surveys since 1972.

The Roper surveys spurred controversy primarily on methodological grounds. Over the years, some communication scholars have questioned the manner in which the "main source" question is asked, whether it is appropriate to the subject matter, and whether it can be answered accurately. As a self-report measure, it asks where people think they get most of their news, and such measures are frequently, though not always, misleading or distorted.

Without dismissing such methodological details, the evidence remains overwhelming that television is now the public's main source of information about **international affairs**. Consider the following:

- The public may prefer one news medium as a source of information about **local** affairs and another one for information about **international** affairs. Such differences should be considered in wording survey questions. The Roper question, by mentioning "the world," makes it more likely that respondents would infer that it deals with international or national affairs rather than with local occurrences. In a 1970 comparative study of Yugoslavia and the United States, Professor Alex S. Edelstein and colleagues allowed respondents from the two nations to suggest which world and local problems were most important to them, then questioned them about the utility of different information sources in dealing with those problems. Even at that date, relatively early in the transformation of global television, respondents in both nations judged television to be a more useful source of information for world problems than for local problems.

- American newspapers tend to be local in character, with a relatively small proportion of international news. The major exceptions would be such elite press as *The New York Times*, *The Washington Post*, *The Los Angeles Times* and *The Christian Science Monitor*, which are read by a small minority of the public. Network television, on the other hand, is predominantly a national and international medium, with nearly half of all stories and available time devoted to international news in recent years. Despite recent trends, most local television stations still rely heavily on the networks for international news.

The impact of such patterns of international news availability was confirmed in a 1985 survey commissioned by the American Society of Newspaper Editors. When questioned about their preferred sources for different types of news, 50 percent of respondents said television was their preferred source for local news, compared with 57 percent who preferred it for state news, and 72 percent who identified it as their preferred source for national and international news. By contrast, 36 percent preferred newspapers for local news, 33 percent for state news, and only 18 percent for national and international news.

- Television has a relatively greater impact than newspapers in conveying news of international affairs. To paraphrase the adage: To what extent is a moving, immediate television picture from a distant location worth a thousand newspaper article words that evening or the next morning? Especially in terms of its political and policy impact, television's ability to convey a sense of reality that is more complete, vivid, emotive and valid than newspapers helps to explain its importance as a source of information. Of course, the print media remain important, especially to certain segments of the public. A 1986 study by a Washington, D.C., public relations firm showed that U.S. senators and representatives cited newspapers, magazines and other print sources 1,504 times in floor speeches, as against 37 mentions of radio and television sources.

- "Saturation coverage" is a recurrent phenomenon of television news. It occurs when a major event occupies all or most of the available airtime. Although television has frequently been called an "electronic front page," that analogy is misleading and fundamentally flawed. Because television broadcasts, in contrast with newspapers, are organized in terms of time rather than space, certain major events and crises tend to saturate available airtime on regular broadcasts and even spill over into special news programs, forcing out other news items that might have been reported. For example, the three networks devoted more than 90 percent of early evening news airtime to the assassination of Egypt's President Sadat on the day it occurred, October 6, 1981. The following evening the story occupied 71 percent of available time, with declining proportions thereafter. By contrast, the timing and absence of network cameras dictated short reports on the first day of the *Achille Lauro* cruise ship hijacking. After devoting 74 percent of airtime to the story on its second day, networks decreased the coverage somewhat for two days, then raised it to 74 percent again when U.S. planes forced an Egyptian plane carrying the hijackers to land at a U.S. base in Italy.

The hijacking of TWA Flight 847 en route from Cairo to Rome in June 1985 is perhaps the best example to date of saturation coverage. About 50 Americans were among the passen-

"Owing to cutbacks in our news department, here is Rod Ingram to guess at what happened today in a number of places around the globe."

Drawing by Dana Fradon; © 1987
The New Yorker Magazine, Inc.

gers held hostage for 16 days. There was intense competition among the networks. In addition to their early evening broadcasts, CBS, ABC and NBC broadcast numerous specials and frequently interrupted regular programming for short updates. CNN concentrated almost entirely on the story. A study of the entire 16 days of the hijacking revealed that ABC devoted an average of 68 percent of its *World News Tonight* broadcast to the story, compared with 62 percent for the *CBS Evening News,* and 63 percent for the *NBC Nightly News.* On four separate nights, ABC spent approximately 90 percent or more of airtime on the story.

During such periods of saturation coverage, public behavior and attitudes toward the media change in important respects. In the midst of heavy network television attention to the Iran hostage crisis in 1980, the Roper organization modified its standard survey question to ask respondents where they had been getting most of their news "about the crisis regarding the U.S. hostages being held in Iran..." and found that 77 percent mentioned television versus only 26 percent who cited newspapers. The Iran case reflected another, more general pattern—that during heavy saturation coverage, the size of already large audiences for television news increases. Their approval rating of the media also rises, according to a massive study of the press during the TWA hostage crisis conducted by the Gallup Organization for The Times Mirror Company. The study showed that people expressed more-positive opinions about the press during the crisis than they did two months after it. In particular, network news "favorability" decreased from 89 percent during the crisis to 82 percent after it. A later survey for Times Mirror found that 75 percent of the public gave favorable ratings to the job TV news has done in covering terrorist incidents, compared with 74 percent who gave the same ratings to newspapers and magazines. Among those who "closely followed" six events—the Pan American Flight 73 hijacking, the Chernobyl nuclear accident, the *Achille Lauro* hijacking, the TWA Flight 847 hostage crisis, the U.S.-Libyan air war and the explosion of the space shuttle Challenger—the proportion of the public giving broadcast and print press favorable ratings ranged from 72 percent to 90 percent.

While the best available evidence suggests that television is indeed the main source of international news for the American public, in particular during major crises, views differ on how much and what kind of information the public is actually acquiring; how well it is understood by individuals; how it is diffused through the public; and how it affects behavior or decisions.

International Concerns

Although the focus of discussion here is on **American** television and foreign policy, the international dimensions are a key to a better understanding of the new relationship of television and foreign policy. New technologies for gathering and disseminating television news are inherently international, rendering control of information by individual governments difficult and sometimes impossible. The Chernobyl nuclear reactor accident is a graphic example. Furthermore, the costs of international news coverage, together with the need for commercial networks to offer a service that is different from that of local affiliates, are pushing them toward seeking to expand the number of cooperative arrangements they have with broadcasting organizations in other nations. (In this area, the economic imperative may break down the strong past reluctance to use "second source" video.) And they are also trying to market their own news programs overseas. In February 1987, the *CBS Evening News* with Dan Rather was offered for the first time in France on Canal Plus, a UHF-TV national subscription channel. The French-subtitled version of the program was shown between seven and eight A.M. Paris time. By midyear, NBC News was planning to send its entire lineup of news programs to hotel rooms on the European continent through the AngloVision satellite channel. Both these developments came more than a year after CNN introduced its programming to European audiences. In December 1984, Edward M. Joyce, then CBS News president, was quoted as saying, "We're looking toward the time in the not-too-distant future when we will be an international news presence, as we are a domestic news presence. In the decade ahead, [Canadian educator Marshall] McLuhan's global village will have arrived, and we see ourselves as a software contributor for it."

The relationship of television and foreign policy has been brought home to both U.S. policymakers and media representatives by the debate over a New World Information and Communication Order. Beginning in the early 1970s, Third World nations led criticism of current international communication structures and the resulting quantity and quality of information flow in the world. They have complained that the dominance of Western media, including wire services, newsfilm and television news organizations, brings disproportionate attention to the larger developed nations and a correspondingly out-of-proportion focus on crisis news and the unusual or the exotic in the Third World. The debate over the future world information order raises questions about the free flow of information across national boundaries, governmental control of news media, appropriate news selection criteria, and the very definition of news itself. Many of the questions are politically and ideologically tinged. Given the current pace of change in the world, they appear likely to intensify rather than abate.

3

Window on the World

The world that we have to deal with politically is out of reach, out of sight, out of mind. It has to be explored, reported and imagined.
—Walter Lippmann, **Public Opinion**, 1921

Broadly conceived, television's role as an observer includes all of the activities involved in gathering and disseminating news relating to foreign policy. The background and training of television news personnel, routine organizational imperatives, standard news selection criteria, economic or technological considerations and the nature of international news content itself are all germane to the observer role. Among these elements, content is perhaps the most crucial. Differences in content imply both a variety of shaping influences and constraints on television as well as mixed effects on the foreign policy process. The problem of defining "news," let alone "international news," is no mean task. In an earlier HEADLINE SERIES on "News From Abroad and the Foreign Policy Public," the authors devoted an entire chapter to the question of what constitutes international news. Even most of the seasoned electronic and print journalists experience some difficulty when asked to define it. (Variations on such tautological definitions as "news is the reporting of change" are frequently heard.) International news itself is not a static phenomenon.

Scholars and other observers note that television is a principal catalyst in the general international debate over the structure of news systems and the flow of news in no small part because of its continued redefinition of news in a way that powerfully relates to foreign policy. One aspect of this redefinition is the increased use of satellite television for communication involving elected officials, nongovernmental policy elites, hijackers or terrorists, and hostages. Another is the new visual vantage point that remote-sensing pictures bring to television news stories. When the focus is on "international," "foreign" or "world" news, there is a strong ideological component involved. As already noted, some representatives of Third World and Communist nations argue for a fundamental redefinition of what constitutes news, moving away from the heavy stress on events, hard news or crises, to a more inclusive definition that would encompass reporting on "development news." Such news often involves slow processes in areas like health, education and agriculture, rather than the fast-breaking, visually compelling "hard news" events to which television is currently attracted.

Scholars have suggested that international news needs to be broken down into subcategories. For example, some researchers with an interest in the media-foreign policy relationship have suggested that foreign policy should be viewed as a separate category within international news. In their view, international news looks at all nations in general, while foreign policy news has to do more specifically with the policy actions and interactions of nations. The problem with a narrow or restrictive definition of foreign policy news is in determining, especially over the long term, what news is relevant to a particular policy initiative or interaction.

A broad and practical definition of international news as it appears on U.S. network television is any news story that involves a country other than the United States, regardless of its theme or place of origin. Such an approach encompasses international news that originates overseas as well as the significant volume emanating from Washington, D.C. It is also appropriate for an era in which satellite interconnections are making the point of origination less important than the identity of the participants in a televised dialogue.

During the 10 years from 1972 through 1981, an average of 7 out of 17 news stories on weeknight network news broadcasts were international items, and they occupied about 10 of the total 22 minutes of airtime available. Such statistics verify the strong international character of network television.

Major Story Formats

During the 1970s, international news items on U.S. network television almost always appeared in one of three formats, each of which bears a significant relationship to the television newsgathering process. One conventional format is the anchor report. Such reports are delivered by the anchor correspondent from the studio location where the broadcast originates, usually New York City or Washington, D.C., but sometimes other U.S. or overseas locations. They are often accompanied by still photos, maps, sketches or diagrams.

The networks rely heavily on the wire services for anchor reports. A 1975 study of the U.S. television networks showed that three quarters or more of the anchor reports broadcast on both domestic and foreign topics were gleaned from the major wire services, principally the Associated Press (AP) and United Press International (UPI). Occasionally, *The New York Times*, *The Washington Post* or other elite media serve this purpose.

In the 10 years from 1972 through 1981, 42 percent of all international news items broadcast by ABC, CBS and NBC on their weeknight broadcasts were anchor reports which averaged 31 seconds in length.

Another conventional format for international news on network television is the domestic video report. Such reports entail visual newsgathering by network correspondents and camera personnel. Although in principle they may originate from any location within the United States, in practice a very high proportion report from such familiar Washington, D.C., sources as the White House, State Department, Department of Defense or the Congress. Relatively few reports originate from the United

Nations in New York or other locations around the country, and even these are frequently tied to presidential travel, such as President Reagan's vacations at his California ranch.

In short, domestic video reports are a good indicator of the close relationship between the U.S. government agenda, especially within the executive branch, and television coverage of international affairs. They represent a phenomenon identified in studies of television news broadcasting in other nations as "foreign news at home." The importance of this category of news has increased in recent years as the result of continued changes in television newsgathering technology. One of the best examples to date is the Iran-contra arms scandal, first news of which broke during the fall of 1986. This news is as thoroughly international as one could imagine; yet a large part of what American audiences hear and see about the events comes out of Washington, D.C. From 1972 through 1981, 26 percent of all international news broadcast by the U.S. networks consisted of domestic video reports, averaging approximately two minutes in length.

A third format for international news is the foreign video report. This represents visual newsgathering at overseas locations by correspondents and camera personnel. In the 1960s and 1970s, nearly all such reports on the U.S. networks were gathered by their own staff. More recently, there has been a trend toward greater use of second-source video, which may come either from individual news organizations or from larger newsfilm (here video) entities, such as WTN (Worldwide Television News) and Visnews.

Some foreign video reports—the "home news abroad" variety—are generated as a direct result of travel by the President or other high U.S. government officials, rather than events in other nations. Others, which might be called "genuine foreign news," consist of reports about events in other nations that do not involve or mention the United States. Examples might be a volcano eruption on a Japanese island, a flood in Bangladesh, a military coup in some nation of the world, or a peaceful transfer of power through elections. During the 10 years from 1972 to 1981, foreign video reports comprised 32 percent of international news on the

U.S. networks, with such reports averaging about two minutes in length.

In the 1980s still another format has appeared with greater frequency on the network early evening news broadcasts. It is the interactive anchor interview with one or more individuals, pioneered by the *MacNeil/Lehrer Report* and *ABC News Nightline*, in which the anchor correspondent conducts a live or taped interview with policymakers, experts or television correspondents in the United States or abroad. The increased use of the interactive anchor interview in international affairs coverage is partly an attempt to offer something different, in more depth and with more context, than local station affiliates.

Trends in Coverage

From the early 1970s, anchor reports, which accounted for half or more of all international news stories in 1972-74, decreased steadily until they accounted for only about 30 percent of such news in 1981. On the other hand, over the same period the proportion of both domestic and foreign video reports increased. The increases occurred during a time of expansion in satellite communication and improvements in transportation and other communication technologies. How the networks used their new technological and economic capabilities is apparent in the attention they devoted to certain nations and regions of the world. A review of *ABC News Nightline* program titles and transcripts shows that nearly half of all broadcasts during 1985 and 1986 dealt with international affairs or foreign policy issues, and, although the topics covered a broad range, several received special emphasis. In March 1985 *Nightline* originated from South Africa for one week, and on numerous other occasions both the internal policies of that country and U.S. policy toward it were the subject of programs. In April 1985, *Nightline* joined a large contingent of other network reporters who broadcast from Vietnam on the 10th anniversary of the end of the Vietnam War. In June 1985, the hijacking of TWA Flight 847 prompted 12 consecutive programs on the hijacking itself and more-general issues relating to terrorism and hostage situations. In October the hijacking of the

Table I: Coverage of 50 Most Frequently Mentioned Nations, 1972–81, Expressed as a Percentage of Sampled International Stories

Nation	ABC Rank	ABC % of Stories	CBS Rank	CBS % of Stories	NBC Rank	NBC % of Stories
United States	1	57.0	1	60.5	1	58.8
U.S.S.R.	2	16.7	2	17.1	2	16.2
Israel	3	14.3	3	13.4	3	13.6
Britain[a]	4	9.8	4	9.9	5	8.8
South Vietnam[b]	5	9.1	5	8.7	4	9.0
Iran	6	8.7	6	8.5	8	7.4
Egypt	7	7.7	7	7.7	6	8.0
North Vietnam	8	7.5	9	7.1	7	7.8
France	9	6.2	8	7.2	9	6.3
China, People's Republic	10	5.3	10	4.6	10	4.6
Lebanon	11	4.2	12	3.9	17	3.0
West Germany	12	4.1	11	4.4	11	4.0
Japan	13	4.1	14	3.4	15	3.2
Syria	14	3.5	13	3.5	13	3.2
Cuba	15	3.2	15	3.2	14	3.2
Poland	16	3.1	17	2.9	17	3.0
Saudi Arabia	17	2.9	13	3.5	12	3.3
Italy	18	2.8	20	2.3	16	3.1
Kampuchea	18	2.8	16	3.1	18	3.0
Afghanistan	19	2.3	29	1.4	23	1.5
Zimbabwe	20	2.2	21	2.2	25	1.3
South Africa	21	2.2	18	2.7	22	1.7
Northern Ireland	22	2.1	26	1.6	23	1.5
Canada	23	1.8	19	2.6	19	2.3
Iraq	24	1.8	30	1.3	27	1.2
Turkey	25	1.6	27	1.5	27	1.2
Jordan	25	1.6	24	1.8	26	1.3
Switzerland	26	1.4	19	2.6	24	1.4
Libya	26	1.4	25	1.7	26	1.3
Mexico	27	1.4	23	1.9	21	1.8
South Korea	28	1.3	22	1.9	20	2.1
India	29	1.3	31	1.1	28	1.1
Spain	30	1.2	26	1.6	25	1.3
Pakistan	30	1.2	35	0.9	33	0.8
Panama	30	1.2	28	1.4	35	0.7
Cyprus	31	1.1	33	1.0	31	0.9
Greece	31	1.1	30	1.3	25	1.3
The Philippines	32	1.0	36	0.8	34	0.8
Thailand	33	1.0	34	1.0	24	1.4
The Vatican	33	1.0	35	0.9	29	1.1
The Netherlands	34	0.9	37	0.8	35	0.7
Algeria	34	0.9	35	0.9	36	0.7
Angola	34	0.9	35	0.9	34	0.8
Laos	34	0.9	41	0.6	30	1.0
Uganda	34	0.9	35	0.9	32	0.9
Portugal	35	0.8	32	1.1	30	1.0
Austria	36	0.8	40	0.7	37	0.7
Argentina	37	0.8	37	0.8	38	0.6
Nicaragua	38	0.7	40	0.7	37	0.7

(continued on next page)

cruise ship *Achille Lauro*—a short-lived event by comparison with the TWA hijacking—brought six consecutive programs. The November 1985 Geneva summit meeting of President Reagan and Soviet leader Mikhail S. Gorbachev received four days of coverage. After two broadcasts on the Philippines in October 1985, *Nightline* turned its attention to that country in early 1986. In February, the program originated from Manila for several days following the Philippine presidential election. During the remainder of 1986, *Nightline* aired additional follow-up broadcasts on the Philippines, along with many on South Africa and a series of programs on the Chernobyl nuclear accident in the Soviet Union. During late 1986 and early 1987, numerous programs were devoted to the unfolding Iran-contra arms scandal.

Perhaps the most striking overall pattern in network television's coverage of international news is its congruence with the foreign policy priorities of the U.S. government. The pattern generally holds whether one looks at coverage of individual nations or at coverage of major geographical regions of the world. Television, like other major media, gives heavy coverage to a small number of nations that somehow directly involve American interests. As shown in Table I, the most frequently covered nations are those involved in major wars or conflicts affecting the United States. These include all of the combatants in the Vietnam War and in the 1973 Middle East war and Iran, because of the

	ABC		CBS		NBC	
Nation	Rank	% of Stories	Rank	% of Stories	Rank	% of Stories
Chile	38	0.7	34	1.0	34	0.8
Sweden	38	0.7	33	1.0	38	0.6
East Germany	38	0.7	38	0.8	33	0.8
Taiwan	39	0.6	39	0.7	34	0.8
Belgium	40	0.6	40	0.7	33	0.8
Number of stories		2,377		2,391		2,286

[a] Excludes Northern Ireland.
[b] After the year 1976, all references to Vietnam were coded as North Vietnam.
Note: Rankings are based on the absolute number of stories in which each nation was mentioned. Due to rounding, nations with different ranks may appear to be cited in the same percentage of sampled stories. Nations are listed in the order of their rank on ABC. More than 50 nations are included in the table because of differences across networks. Percentages sum to more than 100 percent because multiple nations may be mentioned in a single news story.

prolonged hostage crisis. Another group of nations that receive relatively heavy coverage are such political or economic world powers as the U.S.S.R., Britain, France, the People's Republic of China, West Germany and Japan.

Network television shows a similar pattern of attention to the regions of the world. Western Europe, the Middle East and Asia all received relatively high levels of coverage during the 1972-81 period. (Coverage of Asia was elevated in 1972-75 as the result of U.S. involvement in Vietnam.) Network references to the Soviet Union were consistently numerous, but the nations of Eastern Europe, Latin America and sub-Saharan Africa were mentioned infrequently.

The decade-long pattern of independent visual newsgathering by the networks can be seen in Table II on page 37, which shows the proportion of foreign video reports originating from each region on ABC and CBS. They devote by far the greatest effort to covering Western Europe, followed by the Middle East, with Asia a rather distant third. Eastern Europe, including the Soviet Union, Africa and Asia are the "blind spots" in the networks' attempts to provide visual coverage from around the world.

Saturation Coverage

Saturation coverage by television deserves special attention because it distinguishes television's role as an observer of international affairs from that of other media and because television may function differently as a participant or catalyst in foreign policy at times of saturation coverage. Most instances of saturation coverage directly involve the United States or its foreign policy concerns, and in a high proportion of cases there is a major conflict or crisis involving the U.S. government or its citizens, for example, a terrorist incident.

Such heavy coverage is more likely when the networks can tap correspondents from their major overseas bureaus as well as reporters based in Washington, D.C., and New York, and when foreign governments or politico-military conditions do not interfere with the gathering and transmission of news. In November 1979, a major terrorist incident took place at the holiest shrine of

Islam in Mecca, Saudi Arabia. However, it received relatively limited coverage, in part because of strict Saudi government restrictions. The U.S. networks were forced to fall back on artists' sketches, maps and diagrams as a backdrop to much of their coverage.

An important correlate of television's penchant for saturation coverage of hard news is the production, over longer periods of

Table II
Origin of Foreign Video Reports (percentage) on ABC and CBS by Region, 1972-81

Region	ABC	CBS	Both Networks*
Western Europe	41.6	35.8	39.0
Middle East	23.1	25.9	24.3
Asia	15.6	17.4	16.4
Eastern Europe	8.6	7.0	7.9
Latin America	5.4	5.9	5.6
Africa	5.3	5.2	5.2
Canada	0.6	2.7	1.8
Number of stories	841	698	1,539

*Column percentages may not sum to 100 percent because of rounding.

time, of accounts that are episodic and may ignore important historical trends. Iran provides one of the best examples. For almost six years, from 1972 through 1977, there was scarcely any television coverage of Iran, and what there was stressed U.S. arms sales and the importance of that nation as a supplier of oil to the West. From late 1977 through January 1979, coverage continued at a very low level, but there was some attention to growing opposition to Shah Mohammad Reza Pahlavi. Coverage increased briefly as the shah departed Iran and Ayatollah Khomeini returned to take power. Then, from February 1979 until the seizure of hostages at the American embassy, coverage slipped to low levels. Iran, for all practical purposes, dropped from view.

Video: Time Versus Space

Television news, like newspaper news, is presented in narrative form, but the structure is drastically different. Television news is far more coherently organized and tightly unified than newspaper news, both at the level of individual stories and at the level of complete news broadcasts. The classic "inverted pyramid" structure of the newspaper story, with a headline and lead paragraph which convey the broad picture followed by an enumeration of details, is designed to be read in part or in full. Television news stories, on the other hand, are organized in time rather than space. They are expected to exhibit the characteristics of drama and are meant to be viewed in their entirety. The commercial television news broadcast as a whole is similarly structured, in part out of concern for maintaining the viewing audience.

Newspapers and television also differ in the manner in which they narrate accounts of events. The impersonal narrative voice of newspapers stands in stark contrast to the intensely personal narration by television news reporters. This narrative style conveys a sense of the reporter's omniscience, encouraging viewers to have an exaggerated sense of how much it is possible to know about the world. Television also attaches far greater importance to spectacle. Events that can be spectacularly taped are more likely to be covered by television. As one authority has noted, television emphasizes ritual, ceremony and holiday in national and international politics. By making such events as the moon landings, Pope John Paul II's visits, Sadat's visit to Jerusalem, and the Olympics accessible to a vast global audience, television produces a sense of occasion not possible through print media and radio alone.

Technology and News Content

As already noted, satellite, microelectronics, video and transportation technologies are important influences on television and foreign policy. As such, they help to shape the television news message. For example, new technology now allows the U.S. television networks to change their anchor locations with relative ease from New York City to other locations inside or outside the country. When both the *NBC Nightly News* and *ABC World News Tonight* were anchored from Manila during the Philippine election in February 1986, the change in the visual backdrop of the anchor location provided a sense of immediacy that only television, among major news media, is able to convey. The broadcasts also probably contained more news of developments in the Philippines than they would have had they been anchored from New York. In part, this reflected an effort by the networks to maximize the return on their investment and to take advantage of the newsgathering opportunity offered by their presence in the Philippines. On the day of the Philippine presidential election (February 6, 1986, in the United States), *ABC World News Tonight* was anchored by Peter Jennings in Manila and contained reports by correspondents James Laurie in Manila, James Walker in Savao and Mark Litke at Clark Air Base.

The Bottom Line

Economic realities also help to frame television's view of the world. As previously mentioned, the costs of maintaining permanent network bureaus overseas limit the number of nations and regions which enjoy such a presence. In 1982 an executive producer at ABC estimated the cost of maintaining even a "shoestring" bureau overseas at over $1 million per year.

During the 1970s the U.S. commercial networks maintained permanent bureaus in nine nations: Britain, France, West Germany, Italy, U.S.S.R., Lebanon, Israel, Egypt and Japan. Each network also had a permanent bureau in Vietnam until the U.S. withdrawal in April 1975. A quantitative analysis by the author of network television's international news coverage for the 10-year period from 1972 to 1981 showed that both network bureau presence and the location of AP or UPI correspondents were predictors of television's international news coverage. Of these, the presence of a permanent network bureau was a far stronger predictor. Such allocation of personnel and resources by the network news organizations and the wire services upon which they depend outweighed the purely technical consideration of availability of Intelsat satellite earth stations. This relationship held true for nations with large and small populations and high or low gross national product per capita—two factors which were statistically controlled in the analysis.

Organizational Practices

The U.S. networks' present approach to covering international affairs in most parts of the world is described as "parachute journalism," or the "firehouse model" of journalism. When a coup, an earthquake or some other crisis occurs in a distant corner of the globe, network reporters and camera personnel respond much like firefighters as they rush to the scene and, figuratively speaking, parachute in to cover the event. Examples abound. In March 1982, when a military coup overthrew the government of Guatemala, television coverage followed its characteristic pattern. None of the networks had correspondents on the scene at the time, so significant coverage was effectively delayed for a day while they flew in from New York or Miami.

The practice of parachute journalism has been widely criticized. Such network news professionals as John Chancellor of NBC and the late CBS correspondent Charles Collingwood note the loss of depth and context that is intrinsic to this new style of reporting. In the early days of television, more foreign correspondents were expected to acquire a thorough grasp of the politics, history, culture and language of the country in which they were stationed. With today's peripatetic style of reporting, that expectation is sharply diminished.

The news practices of today's jet-set correspondents are in part the product of a quarter century or more of steady change in the background, training and interests of television correspondents. In his study of foreign affairs correspondents for television, Robert M. Batscha found that among correspondents hired before 1963, 49 percent had a newspaper background and 38 percent came from a television background. Among those hired after 1963, the proportion was reversed, with 48 percent coming from a television background and only 38 percent from newspaper work. This general trend has continued, with increasing emphasis on the importance of a television background and training.

Other research, such as John C. Pollock's 1981 book on *The Politics of Crisis Reporting*, which was based on interviews with 102 print and electronic journalists who covered Latin America, suggests another important characteristic of foreign correspondents. About six out of ten indicated that the challenges of professional newsgathering, rather than an interest in Latin America as a region, explained why they liked such reporting.

The perils of parachute journalism were tragically illustrated in the case of ABC television correspondent Bill Stewart, who was sent from the network's New York bureau in June 1979 to cover the war in Nicaragua. Although Stewart had previously reported from Iran, even his colleagues noted that he was inappropriately trained for reporting from Latin America. He spoke no Spanish and had no background in the region. Consequently, Stewart hired as an assistant a young Nicaraguan who was suspected of being a Sandinista. The youth was apprehended and shot at a government roadblock, and moments later correspondent Stewart was executed. The entire episode was videotaped by Stewart's cameraman, and all three U.S. television networks later broadcast footage of the shooting.

News Values

Closely related to organizational considerations is the question of news values. In one important sense, news values may be thought of as news-selection criteria, those qualities of events that determine their selection for broadcast from among the myriad possibilities available to a television news organization. In another sense, news values are guidelines that tell the television journalist what to include, emphasize or omit in the treatment of a particular story.

Researchers have identified a number of values that influence the selection of news by the media. For television they include drama, visual attractiveness, entertainment, size or importance of the story, cultural or geographical proximity, negativity, recency, and involvement with elite nations or individuals.

Some of these values relate to the narrative structure of television news, which contrasts sharply with that of print news. The television story is structured in time, with the anchor or correspondent serving as a highly personal storyteller who gives a unified interpretation to the ideas. More importantly, it is presented through the **visual images**. A "good" television news story often contains rising and falling action or spectacular visual elements that hold audience attention. Other news values, such as involvement with elite nations or individuals, relate more directly to the structure of television news organizations. All of the commercial networks maintain a heavy presence in Washington, D.C., and place their overseas bureaus predominantly in Western Europe and other major capitals.

Government influence on television's role as an observer of international affairs may take many different forms. The predominant ones are censorship and "news management," although measures such as the licensing of journalists have the support of some governments and are periodically debated in international meetings. A recent example of censorship is the government of South Africa's imposition of restrictions on the activities of all news organizations, with special attention to television news.

The practice of news management refers to the coordinated or strategic use of the media by government officials as news sources, principally the President and other officials within the executive branch, in an effort to shape the content of media coverage. The success of news management derives in part from the prevalence of what historian and former Librarian of Congress Daniel Boorstin, in his book *The Image*, called pseudo-events. Such events may include press conferences, briefings, speeches, presidential travel and the like. They are usually planned rather than spontaneous, and have the immediate purpose of generating media coverage. Their relationship to the underlying reality of a situation is often ambiguous and they are frequently intended to be self-fulfilling prophecies.

While the practice of news management does not require a Machiavellian interpretation of any President or Administration, it is a persistent and ever more widely recognized form of governmental influence on television coverage. In Boorstin's polemic, the arrival of around-the-clock media such as television accelerated the flood of pseudo-events. The question of how television, with its relentless visual immediacy, might enhance government influence on media is of growing importance.

4

Television 'Diplomacy'

Even before the advent of global television, scholars recognized that the press acts as a participant in the foreign policy process by providing the view of reality that is most often and most heavily relied upon by government officials as a basis for policy decisions. It also acts as a recipient and conveyor of various official contributions to news content. With new uses of television technology, a third role has been added which more sharply distinguishes television from the other major media—that of direct participant in the policy process. Television provides an interactive channel for diplomacy which is instantaneous or timely and in which journalists frequently assume an equal role with officials in the diplomatic dialogue.

Although government officials have access to numerous sources of information, including private diplomatic channels, it is well known that they rely most heavily on the public news media for their view of events around the world. As W. Phillips Davison of Columbia University noted more than a decade ago, it is only a slight exaggeration to say that the mass media are the eyes and ears of diplomacy. Top policymaking officials of the U.S. government pay close attention to *The New York Times* and *The Washington Post*. They also have access to the wire services and to specially prepared summaries of the day's news from selected print and broadcast media. Even government intelligence agencies devote the bulk of their effort to monitoring and interpreting news media output around the world. One example of such effort is the Foreign Broadcast Information Service (FBIS) of the U.S. government, which tapes, translates and transcribes selected output of broadcast news from around the world. Formerly part of the CIA, FBIS remains a quasi-intelligence arm of the U.S. government.

In recent years, the President and other high policymaking officials of the government have become much more highly attuned to television news. President Lyndon B. Johnson displayed a strong personal interest in the medium and had three television monitors installed side by side in the Oval Office of the White House so that he could simultaneously keep track of what all three major networks covered. President Nixon and succeeding Presidents have apparently relied more heavily on regular written summaries of press output, including television. However, the testimony of top policymakers in all recent U.S. Administrations agrees strongly on one point: regular monitoring of television news coverage has become as essential as consistent reading of the elite printed press.

Alexander M. Haig Jr. reported in a March 1985 article for *TV Guide* that when he was White House chief of staff, deputy national security adviser, supreme allied commander of the North Atlantic Treaty Organization and secretary of state, his first order of business each morning was to look at the previous evening's network television news content. Haig also noted that when Israel invaded Lebanon in 1982, President Reagan was so appalled by the killing and destruction on television that he phoned Israeli Prime Minister Menachem Begin requesting a halt to the bombing.

The President and other top policymakers have several closely related reasons for the new attention to television. They want to see which of their own statements or actions are covered by television and in what manner. Careful attention to television output enables them to respond more quickly to reports they perceive as incomplete or inaccurate. Officials attend to television news to see and hear what other policy elites, including members of Congress or leaders of foreign governments, are saying. Although the print media will also report such statements, usually in greater detail, the immediacy of television often makes it a preferred channel for diplomatic and policy dialogue.

Policymakers work on the assumption that television is far more influential politically than the other news media. Its influence is conventionally attributed to its large outreach, immediacy and visual impact.

Under certain circumstances, such as terrorist attacks or hostage situations that demand rapid policy decisions or reaction, the immediacy of television heightens its importance. Crisis-management teams in the White House, State Department or other government agencies may monitor television news particularly closely, along with other available sources, for information on breaking stories. According to Edward Joyce, CBS had access to information that had not yet reached the U.S. government during the first 48 hours of the hijacking of TWA Flight 847 in June 1985. Recounting the circumstances in a 1986 issue of the *SAIS Review*, Joyce noted that "A State Department official reacted with horrified disbelief when told by CBS News that the hijackers had separated and removed hostages with Jewish-sounding names."

News Management

Scholars who have studied the media-foreign policy relationship, and more particularly the relationship between news reporters and governmental officials, agree on the importance of various official contributions to the media. These include press conferences, news releases, background briefings, leaks and even covert "disinformation" campaigns. The actions of government officials, in addition to what they say or the information they provide, can affect the volume and nature of news conveyed through television and other media. Summit diplomacy is perhaps the best example of this phenomenon. When President Reagan met with Gorbachev in Geneva in November 1985, the U.S. commercial networks sent hundreds of personnel there to cover the summit and shifted anchor locations for the purpose.

Most observers and students of the government-media relationship also concur on the importance of voluntary versus involuntary contributions to the media. In his book, *Reporters and Officials*, Leon V. Sigal differentiates among **routine channels** such as official proceedings, press releases, press conferences and nonspontaneous events; **informal channels** such as background briefings, leaks, nongovernmental proceedings or other news reports; and **enterprise channels**, including interviews, spontaneous events, books, research or the reporter's own analysis. In a study of *The New York Times* and *The Washington Post* spanning 20 years, from 1949 through 1969, he documented a pattern of heavy reliance on routine and informal channels. They accounted for 58.2 percent and 15.7 percent of the channels used by *The New York Times* and *The Washington Post* respectively in his sample of news stories. Further, he showed that U.S. and foreign government officials were the dominant sources when both routine and informal channels were used, accounting for 84.1 percent of sources for routine and 78.1 percent of sources for informal channels.

How does television news compare with the print media in its pattern of reliance on routine, informal and enterprise channels, especially in coverage of international affairs? Although this question has not been directly addressed in quantitative terms, some rather clearcut evidence suggests that television relies even more than print media on routine and informal channels, with official government sources predominating.

Two decade-long trends in network television's coverage of international affairs support this conclusion. In 1972, domestic video reports originating predominantly from Washington, D.C., increased steadily as a proportion of all network international news coverage, rising from 24 percent to 30 percent in 1981. During the same period, foreign video reports, which include a heavy component of "home news abroad" (travel by the Presi-

Auth © 1983 *The Philadelphia Inquirer*.
Reprinted with permission of Universal Press Syndicate.
All rights reserved.

dent, secretary of state or other officials), also increased from 26 percent of all international news in 1972 to approximately 40 percent of such coverage in 1981.

The coverage reflects the allocation of network resources and the stationing of their correspondents. The White House, State Department and Pentagon are all important and regular sources of foreign policy news. It is axiomatic that when the President and, increasingly, other high-level officials conduct official travel, the television networks will dispatch personnel to cover the event.

The large outreach, immediacy and visual character of television news give it a political impact that cannot be ignored by policymaking officials. Therefore, the President and other top government officials rely on television to convey government policies forcefully and effectively to the public at home and sometimes abroad. Careful planning of travel, press conferences, background briefings and leaks to the press are all part of this form of news management. During the Reagan presidency, efforts to plan and manage daily "photo opportunities" and to coordinate his overall exposure to and use of the press—especially television—have received a new and high priority in the White House. In particular, he has held far fewer press conferences than several television-age Presidents, preferring instead the more-controlled formats of speeches before chosen groups, televised addresses without questions, and regular Saturday radio addresses.

Lloyd Cutler, based on his experience in the Carter White House, suggests that "learning how to adjust to the influence of television is central to the art of governing today." In the design and implementation of foreign policy, policymakers increasingly view the public impact of television and other media as a variable to be considered, controlled and managed in order to have a successful policy. The question of how much control elected and nonelected policy officials **should** seek to exercise over media content and the questions about the degree to which government news-management activities constrict the scope of public policy debate are of increasing concern.

New Forum for Diplomatic Communication

Television's role as a direct channel or forum for diplomacy evolved during the 1970s and early 1980s. Viewers will recall that in November 1977, Walter Cronkite was widely credited with facilitating an agreement between Israeli Prime Minister Begin and Egyptian President Sadat that led to Sadat's historic visit to Israel. Cronkite had conducted separate interviews with the two leaders that were aired together on the same broadcast of the *CBS Evening News*. It is now known that the actual agreement had been worked out through more-traditional channels and that Cronkite and television were simply used to confirm it publicly.

For several weeks immediately following the seizure of American hostages at the U.S. embassy in Tehran during November 1979, television news became a principal channel of communication between the two nations. In his book, *America Held Hostage*, Pierre Salinger, the Paris-based former press secretary to President John F. Kennedy, describes the efforts of the Iranian and U.S. governments to establish some form of direct, nonpublic contact during that initial period. During the ensuing 444 days of the hostage crisis, both governmental and nongovernmental policy elites were to use television in a variety of ways, including as a direct channel for diplomatic communication.

The Genesis of ABC News Nightline

The long Iran hostage crisis provided the opportune time for ABC News to introduce a regular, half-hour late night news program. Capitalizing on viewer interest in the Iran story, the network began a series of regular evening broadcasts, initially titled *America Held Hostage,* and hosted by Frank Reynolds and later Ted Koppel. These drew on a format introduced earlier on PBS in the *MacNeil/Lehrer Report* and quickly evolved into the successful *Nightline* program. Among the advantages *Nightline* possessed over the MacNeil/Lehrer program were the financial resources of a commercial news operation and a larger audience. *Nightline* has evolved into a program which places heavy emphasis on foreign policy issues. Its motto is "Bringing together people who are worlds apart."

The Philippines presents an especially vivid illustration of television's new role as a forum for diplomacy. In the fall of 1985, as the political situation in the Philippines continued to deteriorate, such U.S. television programs as NBC's *Meet the Press* and PBS's *MacNeil/Lehrer Newshour* began devoting more attention to that country, including interviews with President Ferdinand Marcos. On the November 3, 1985, edition of *This Week with David Brinkley,* President Marcos responded to a pointed question from commentator George Will by announcing that he would call for elections within two or three months.

As it turned out, those elections became a watershed in the Philippines and culminated in Marcos' downfall. The U.S. Congress was allowed to send a team of observers, headed by Senator Richard Lugar (R-Ind.), to monitor the election. The senator received a high level of visibility amid the saturation coverage given the election. In addition, U.S. television broadcast interviews with a number of high-level Philippine government and opposition leaders as well as U.S. Administration and congressional leaders. During January and February of 1986 they included such figures as Pacifico Castro, Philippine foreign minister, Blas Ople, the Philippine labor minister sent by Marcos as an emissary to Washington, Representative Stephen J. Solarz (D-N.Y.), chairman of the House Foreign Affairs Committee's subcommittee on Asian and Pacific affairs, and many others. The spotlight of television made it politically much more difficult for the Reagan Administration to continue a policy of supporting the Marcos government in the face of massive voting irregularities and mounting evidence of prior misuse of power and lack of public support within the Philippines.

Although President Marcos' announcement of snap elections came after President Reagan had sent his close friend Senator Paul Laxalt (R-Nev.) to the Philippines to tell Marcos that the President was growing increasingly impatient with the pace of reform, the question as to how much television journalism itself had to do with Marcos' decision persisted and was widely discussed. The following exchange from the April 4, 1986, edition of *Nightline,* in which Ted Koppel interviewed ex-President Marcos in Hawaii, is instructive.

KOPPEL: A few months ago, Mr. President, on my colleague David Brinkley's program you surprised him. I think you surprised almost everyone by announcing a snap election.
MARCOS: I surprised myself too.
KOPPEL: Did you?
MARCOS: Oh, yes. Well, I had thought about it, but I never did think I would make the decision through that medium.
KOPPEL: Did you really do it that instinctively, just like that?
MARCOS: Yes. You could say that I was a little irritated that evening about all these news and the attempt to falsify some evidence on, again, on hidden wealth.

One Institution or Two?

Because at least one anchor and often other journalists participate in these televised discussions linking policymaking elites from two or more nations in a public dialogue, the format poses a central issue in the consideration of "media" or "television" diplomacy. How do the journalists differ from the policymakers in such encounters? Have television journalists assumed a diplomatic rather than just a reporting role?

Another way of posing the issue is to ask whether television news and the policymaking arms of U.S. government might be better conceptualized as a single institution rather than two separate ones. Much has been written about the adversarial relationship of media and government and, more recently, their symbiotic relationship. However, programs like *Nightline* provide evidence that television journalists have moved beyond symbiosis to direct involvement in diplomacy, and diplomats for their part have moved more fully into the public televised realm.

To consider television news and diplomacy as a single institution is not without problems. The institution may appear singular in its technology and the roles of officials and reporters as participants. However, government officials and news media representatives may have competing interests owing to the inherently international and highly politicized nature of media diplomacy. It forces both diplomats and reporters to reconsider the oft-invoked conventional wisdom that, according to patriotic American tradition, politics stop at the water's edge. The contradiction is most apparent to reporters who, on the one hand, must consider traditional canons of objectivity and balance in reporting and, on the other, the prospect that following those time-honored guidelines may damage U.S. foreign policy interests.

5

Public Influence on Foreign Policy

All political systems have their myths, and democracies are not exceptions in this regard. The democratic myth is that the people are inherently wise and just and that they are the real rulers of the republic.

—Gabriel Almond, **The American People and Foreign Policy**, 1950

The American public as a whole does not influence foreign policy in a direct sense. There are sharp gradations of interest and competence in, as well as influence on, foreign policy. A noted authority on public opinion, Almond suggests that the public can be thought of as a pyramid-shaped structure including, from bottom to top, the large general public, a smaller attentive public that is informed about foreign policy problems and forms the audience for discussions among elites, the policy and opinion elites, and, within the elites, the official policy leadership, including executives, legislators and civil servants. Within such a structure, the leadership groups produce foreign policies and carry out policy formulation and advocacy. The public role in the process is to set certain policy criteria in the form of widely held values and expectations. These may be expressed through such formal means as voting, through public opinion polls or, on occasion, through widespread public demonstrations, as in the Vietnam era.

Although the role of the press as a forum for elite dialogue on foreign policy issues predates the contemporary era, television exerts a profound new influence. I.M. Destler, Leslie H. Gelb and Anthony Lake in their 1984 book, *Our Own Worst Enemy: The Unmaking of American Foreign Policy*, suggest that Congress and the media, principally television, have decreased presidential influence and contributed to a breakdown of national consensus in foreign policy. They argue that the real and perceived impact of television has important effects on foreign-policy making. It vastly increases the emphasis given to national versus local political issues. Political candidates increasingly succumb to the temptation to gain national press attention through telegenic statements or pithy "sound bites," in media jargon. The politics of fund-raising, primaries and maneuvering in relation to presidential elections mean that approximately two out of every four years may be characterized by partisan debate over foreign policy issues. Moreover, television's amplification of conflicts in the here and now reduces the ability of an incumbent Administration to determine which foreign policy issues are crucial and which can be downplayed. Live television may also increase the risk of a blunder which may haunt a political leader later on. Haig's statement from the White House that "I'm in control here" might have been quickly forgotten if it had not been spoken on television to a nation alarmed by an attempted assassination of the President.

In *The Kennedy Crises: The Press, the Presidency and Foreign Policy*, Montague Kern, Patricia W. Levering and Ralph B. Levering examined five categories of claimants for public attention in an effort to determine which had greater impact on television's coverage of international affairs, the presidency or the press. In addition to the President and the press, they looked at domestic politicians, foreign sources and interest groups. These five categories are similar to those used in other studies of television coverage of international affairs and they provide a useful and exhaustive list of the major actors in the ongoing televised dialogue on foreign policy. However, all who seek public attention through television are not equal. Most studies demonstrate that it is the foreign policy elites, in and out of government, at home and abroad, who dominate the televised dialogue. This finding shows that television is continuing the propensity of other media coverage of international affairs to focus disproportionately on a narrow group of nations and individuals.

The President and the Executive Branch

Viewers of the major weeknight network news broadcasts, the *CBS Evening News, NBC Nightly News* and *ABC World News Tonight,* regularly see more of the President and the White House than of any other individual or institution covered on television news. Network news producers routinely assume that the actions and words of the President will be of interest to the public, perhaps especially so when they bear on foreign policy or international relations. In addition to the White House, there is a strong supporting cast of characters at the Department of State, the Department of Defense and to a lesser extent at other Federal agencies such as the CIA. Network television's reliance on executive-branch sources helps to explain the ability of that branch of government to control and manage the foreign policy agenda presented to the American public.

Domestic Politicians

Members of Congress and other domestic politicians provide a counterpoint to television's emphasis on the presidency, but their influence is much more sporadic. The foreign policy statements of U.S. senators, representatives or governors receive coverage on television news and in other major media because they characteristically represent opposing points of view. Consequently they possess the news value of conflict while at the same time fulfilling the journalistic criterion of "fairness" or "balance" in coverage of an issue. Moreover, members of Congress are accessible to the television networks. This is especially the case for influential members of Congress, who benefit from the television networks' Capitol Hill correspondents and their large Washington, D.C., bureaus. Some politicians receive coverage because they are powerful in their own right or because they are possible contenders for power. All other things equal, senators may command more airtime than representatives, and certain congressmen such as the chairs of the House Foreign Affairs or Senate Foreign Relations committees may receive greater media attention on foreign policy issues. It is a foregone conclusion that any viable candidate for the presidency will demonstrate some expertise in foreign affairs.

The September 10, 1985, broadcast of *ABC News Nightline* illustrated this dynamic at work. Anchor Ted Koppel in Washington conducted a live interview with Senator Edward M. Kennedy (D-Mass.) in Washington and South African Foreign Minister Pik Botha in Johannesburg. Senator Kennedy led a faction in the U.S. Senate seeking tougher sanctions against South Africa, and sanctions were a focal point of the discussion, which included the following exchanges.

KOPPEL: Well, my point, Senator, is that he has all but joined you. I mean, I think if anyone had predicted three or four months ago that Ronald Reagan was going to come out in favor of the sanctions that he has now enunciated, people would have said you were out of your mind.

KENNEDY: Well, the fact of the matter is that this is too little. This is too late. This action was taken basically to avoid an important defeat in the Senate of the United States, and done so begrudgingly. I don't question the President's motives, but I certainly question the President's policy. I would hope that he would permit the members of the Republican party to be true to the values of Lincoln and not to the values of *apartheid* when we call the roll tomorrow at 4 o'clock.

A later portion of the broadcast included the following excerpted exchange.

BOTHA: . . .I do not believe that these sanctions will achieve anything except to soothe his own conscience and that of some senators and congressmen in the United States because of an internal United States problem. I cannot help, and many of my black friends in this country, black leaders, cannot help, we are discussing this, that you have introduced this issue to defeat President Reagan. You couldn't defeat him on other internal political issues, so you would choose this one, the color issue, which is a dramatic one in the United States. . . .

After Foreign Minister Botha had finished his comment and Senator Kennedy had replied, anchorman Koppel returned to the issue.

KOPPEL: Let me come right back, Senator Kennedy, to you because there was what sounded suspiciously to me like almost a frontal assault on you. It sounded as though the foreign minister was saying what you're doing, you're doing for whatever presidential aspirations you may have, whatever you're doing you're doing for domestic political reasons and not because you care about South Africa. You may have chosen to turn the other cheek on that. If so, we'll gloss by it. But I just wanted to raise it.

BOTHA: But can I just get an opportunity—

KENNEDY: If I could now, Mr. Botha, if I could answer the question. The question isn't about my presidential ambitions or whether I may be elected or not elected president. The issue is, when will a black be able to be elected president of South Africa? And no condemnation of America in the past, of American history or American political leadership, Democrat or Republican alike, can take away from that essential fact. And that is essentially the issue.

Although Senator Kennedy subsequently withdrew from any possible bid for the presidency in 1988, his role on the September 1985 *Nightline* broadcast is one capsule illustration of the fact that media attention to the foreign policy positions of U.S. politicians relates to both their power position and their potential power to challenge the incumbent in the White House. In early 1987, one of the most significant aspects of the Iran-contra arms scandal may well have been its timing, coming at the beginning of maneuvering by candidates interested in the 1988 presidential election.

Foreign Sources

Foreign sources, consisting predominantly of government officials, rank a strong second to U.S. officials and policy elites in televised discussions of foreign policy. The general pattern has been well documented for print media. (See Leon V. Sigal's 1973 study, *Reporters and Officials*.) Kern, Levering and Levering corroborated that finding, but they concluded that foreign sources, although heavily relied upon by the media, were seldom a challenge to the President. Under most circumstances, foreign views were either ignored or taken into account only on a highly selective basis. Given the tendency of media to focus foreign coverage through a domestic prism, it was relatively easy for Americans to ignore or discount the views of Soviet leader Nikita S. Khrushchev, Cuba's Fidel Castro and France's Charles de Gaulle in the cold-war atmosphere of the 1960s.

Today some foreign sources have more direct and immediate access to the American public through television than ever before. Notable examples include Aquino, Nicaragua's Daniel Ortega and the Palestine Liberation Organization's Yasir Arafat.

During the TWA Flight 847 hostage situation, Nabih Berri, leader of the powerful Amal Shiite group in Lebanon, emerged as a principal spokesman and helped to orchestrate a number of events staged especially for television, including interviews with some of the hostages and even a farewell dinner for them at a seaside restaurant in Beirut prior to their release. According to Michael J. O'Neill, Berri moved into the crisis with the smooth assurance of a European diplomat, well dressed and clean shaven. He is a lawyer who regularly visits his former American wife and six children in Dearborn, Michigan.

While such foreign sources may have achieved great public reach and exposure, the question of their impact on policy is much more complex. During the TWA 847 hijacking, O'Neill ventures that pictures of Berri looking like the lawyer that he is, reasonable rather than violent, and shots of the hostages chatting and eating in a chummy restaurant setting may have lowered public fears and reduced pressures on the White House, as some officials conceded. However, this possible influence took place against the backdrop of a dramatic hostage situation. How would Berri's possible influence compare with that of Soviet leader Gorbachev during a summit meeting with President Reagan, Philippine President Aquino addressing a joint session of Congress during a visit to the United States, or Japanese Prime Minister Yasuhiro Nakasone commenting on trade issues during an economic summit meeting in Tokyo? Clearly, it is not only the characteristics of foreign sources themselves, or even the nation or group they represent, but the broader context of international affairs or events within which they appear on U.S. television that affects their possible influence on U.S. policy.

Interest Groups

Organized interest groups representing one cause or another play a lesser though perceptible part in the televised dialogue on foreign policy issues. During the waning years of the Vietnam War an organization called Vietnam Veterans Against the War received some attention on network news. More recently, interest groups have appeared on television news to voice opposition to apartheid in South Africa or support for stronger U.S. sanctions against that nation. Antinuclear interest groups have coalesced around issues of arms control, the Reagan Administration's Strategic Defense Initiative ("Star Wars") and the continuing spread of nuclear weapons.

Representatives of the news media themselves claim a certain degree of attention in the public dialogue on foreign policy issues. Such programs as *Washington Week in Review, This Week with David Brinkley, Face the Nation* and *Meet the Press* exemplify that participation, but it also extends more broadly to include commentary and advocacy journalism on regular newscasts, specials or other programs.

Ample experience and evidence suggest that ordinary members of the general public characteristically play only an incidental role in media coverage of international affairs. When members of the general public do appear on television, they are frequently thrust into the picture by virtue of involvement with a hijacking, hostage situation, earthquake or similar breaking news. During the Iran hostage crisis, all three commercial networks made interviews with wives, mothers or other relatives of the American hostages part of the story within a day or two of the embassy seizure. This strong element of human drama injected at the very beginning of the 444-day captivity made it a difficult facet to ignore as the crisis wore on. The pattern of coverage during the 1979–81 Iran crisis resembled both earlier reporting on American prisoners of war (POWs) in Vietnam and subsequent stories of hostages in Lebanon. The hostages become one focal point of coverage, and their relatives or friends at home, another, if with lesser emphasis. The overall story line traces the pain, suffering and ultimately joy or sadness that permeate the lives of these innocent victims.

Public Opinion and Foreign Policy

According to prevailing thought, mass public opinion operates in an indirect manner by suggesting the outer constraints or limits within which a U.S. Administration can plan and implement its foreign policy. Almond suggested that the three essential criteria of a democratic policymaking process are a formal opportunity for mass participation; genuine autonomy and competition among foreign policy elites; and an informed and interested attentive public before whom elite dialogue takes place.

Scholars of a more critical bent than Almond have suggested that governmental and nongovernmental foreign policy elites tend to agree on goals and only infrequently disagree on tactics. As a

Steve Kelley in the *San Diego Union*.
Reprinted with permission.

result, television and the other major media report within a narrow perspective on matters of foreign policy.

Leaving aside for a moment the question of the range of views or options presented in television coverage of international affairs, how does television's impact on public opinion differ from that of print media?

Television's Immediacy

The very definition of news as a form of knowledge denotes its time value: news is the reporting of "current" events. Contemporary television news possesses a quality of immediacy that clearly distinguishes it from other major news media, enabling it to build awareness of international events more quickly, with consequent pressures on policymakers.

Newspapers, for example, operate on a 24-hour cycle and are circulated on the basis of a morning or evening edition. The older concept of the "extra" newspaper edition died out with the growth of electronic media. Although radio news is timely and accessible, it lacks visual immediacy. The three major network news organizations, ABC, CBS and NBC, also operate on a regular schedule under normal circumstances, with early morning, early evening and late evening news, and short newsbreaks during prime-time evening hours. However, during crises or major events the network news organizations will preempt their regular entertainment programming to carry news bulletins of varying length. For example, the networks carried numerous special reports during the TWA Flight 847 hijacking in 1985. On the other hand, CNN is able to carry continuous, if repetitive, coverage of such crises without concern about preempting commercially lucrative entertainment programs.

Along with scheduling flexibility, television's capacity to build quickly public awareness adds to the sense of immediacy it conveys. Because of their large audiences, any event major enough to receive coverage on all three networks, CNN and Independent Network News (INN) will reach a large segment of the American public.

The testimony of former high-level officials in the executive branch of the U.S. government suggests strongly that the immediacy of television may affect the timing of some policy decisions or at the very least add a sense of urgency to policy deliberations that did not exist before television. Lloyd Cutler has referred to television as a "doomsday clock" and to the "constant drumbeat of TV news."

Compared with the other news media, television is recognized for its capacity to transmit a wide range of human emotions. Close-up camera shots, whether of bombing victims, hostages reading notes from their captors, tearful relatives, presidential speeches or congressional replies, all illustrate this strength of the medium. At the level of a two- or three-minute television news story, the widely accepted standard was articulated in an oft-quoted 1963 memorandum from Reuven Frank, then executive producer of the *NBC Evening News*, to his staff. "Every news story should, without any sacrifice of probity or responsibility, display the attributes of fiction, of drama. It should have structure and conflict, problem and denouement, rising action and falling action, a beginning, a middle and an end. These are not only the essentials of drama; they are the essentials of narrative."

High-Reach Saturation Coverage

Those major events that warrant saturation coverage by television news organizations may have especially powerful political effects because of the sheer size of the audience exposed one or perhaps multiple times to the televised messages. The explosion of the space shuttle Challenger provides an excellent case in point. From the day of the launch disaster, it generated an extended period of saturation television coverage during which the in-flight explosion itself was broadcast numerous times by all major television networks and their affiliates. Many of those same television reports and pictures were relayed instantly to nations all around the world, where they would again be repeatedly telecast. From a policy standpoint, there was special interest among allies in Japan, Western Europe and elsewhere who were cooperating with the U.S. space shuttle program or had satellite launch programs of their own.

The Challenger explosion undermined public confidence here and abroad in U.S. policy concerning the use of manned shuttle flights for satellite launches or civilian ventures into space. In the wake of Challenger, policy decisions relating to space exploration were discussed and made more openly than would have been possible in a pretelevision era.

6

Reform or Radical Redefinition?

A central message of this HEADLINE SERIES is that television's new importance in the media-foreign policy relationship raises issues of vital concern to media, government and public alike. They bear on prospects for a democratic U.S. foreign policy in an era of global television and can only be meaningfully discussed within a broad international context.

How will television's growing capacity as a channel for global communication affect its relationship to the foreign policy process in years to come? The short history of that relationship suggests both the difficulty and the importance of the question. For example, it appears clear that changes in technology are only part of the answer. Despite the capability to broadcast timely visual news from anywhere in the world, U.S. television shows a highly selective pattern of attention, influenced by such factors as government policies, news-management efforts, economics, and the competitive practices of commercial news organizations.

Many government and even nongovernmental entities are

using television for diplomatic communication, either directly or through news-management efforts. Other nations restrict or censor newsgathering, with special attention to television. A large number of countries throughout the world are dissatisfied with the present international flow of visual news precisely because of its presumed impact on foreign policy.

Efforts to suggest or predict future improvements in the media-foreign policy relationship are complicated by two persistent dilemmas that face broadcast news. First, prevailing notions and practices dictate that the news should be as comprehensive as possible, yet for obvious reasons it must also be selective. The second dilemma is that news, while expected to convey objective, factual accounts, is also obliged to make them meaningful to the audience. However, the addition of context and explanation almost inevitably involves the intrusion of opinion and points of view. In the face of these two basic dilemmas, future changes in television news and its relationship to foreign policy must fall somewhere along a continuum ranging from gradual reform to more radical redefinition and organizational restructuring.

Some suggestions for improvements in television coverage of international news have been repeatedly brought to public or industry attention but with little success. One is that news programs, especially the flagship early evening network news broadcasts, be lengthened to permit more explanation, context and depth. Countless television news journalists, including Cronkite and former CBS News President Fred Friendly, have promoted the notion over the years, but it has met with a stiff rebuff, given current economic trends within the U.S. television industry. Local station affiliates of the major networks are simply unwilling to give up valuable commercial time to allow a lengthening of the network news broadcasts. Major commercial networks have contented themselves with short newsbreak inserts during prime time and programs such as *Nightline,* which appears on the late fringe of the commercially lucrative prime time.

One suggestion calls for the elimination of commercials from the existing weeknight network news broadcasts. This would add nearly eight minutes of time for news. Another recommendation is that some or all news broadcasts be exempted from commercial interruption on a regular basis, as is the current practice with some news specials. Commercially supported television systems in other nations show that the U.S. model is not the only viable option. Most European nations, for example, have a history of reluctance to adopt commerical support for public service television which is to convey news, information and education.

Another proposal is to provide fewer stories with more concentration on depth and context. Industry observers note that U.S. networks have made moves in this direction as local affiliates expanded their news time. However, with only 22 minutes available for news on the weeknight network broadcasts, the magazine approach of opting for fewer and more-comprehensive stories inevitably sacrifices breadth of world events coverage, given the large number of nations and breaking events around the world. Any real contribution to depth in international news would require that a high proportion of such magazine-format stories be devoted to world affairs.

International news coverage might also be improved by an increase in numbers of and better training for foreign affairs correspondents. This approach would include an emphasis on area and linguistic expertise for foreign correspondents.

Most, if not all, of the arguments against such training relate once again to the organizational expectations and demands placed on journalists who wish to advance through the ranks of highly competitive commercial news organizations. As Edward J. Epstein perceptively noted in his breakthrough book *News From Nowhere*, the business logic of network television must be understood before one can understand journalistic aspects of the enterprise. As businesses, the major U.S. networks have recently emphasized such qualities as television training, mobility and even "star" quality over area or linguistic expertise.

A closely related recommendation calls for the U.S. television organizations to make a major investment in a more extensive network of permanent bureaus in a conscious effort to reverse the excesses of "parachute journalism." To date, economic logic has supported current practices and discouraged any realistic consideration of such an alternative. Future CBS television coverage of Eastern Europe and Southeast Asia will have to be assessed in light of that organization's removal of the Warsaw and Bangkok bureaus during its latest round of budget cutbacks in early 1987.

Still another suggestion for reform is to increase greatly the practice of "news-pooling," in which the U.S. commercial news organizations lag far behind such enterprises as the Eurovision News Exchange. Improved, more-portable satellite technology is pushing the networks slowly in this direction, and there has already been a perceptible increase in the use of second source video—coverage taped by other organizations but aired by the networks. However, the suggestion for news-pooling flies in the face of present competitive practices by ABC, CBS and NBC. The networks place a very high value on use of their own correspondents and on "scooping" the competition on a story. They chafe at the notion of pooling arrangements, even on a limited basis in crisis situations.

During the hijacking of TWA Flight 847, ABC, CBS and NBC were unable to agree among themselves to pool coverage of interviews with the passengers held hostage. Richard C. Wald, senior vice-president of ABC News, cited several reasons why pooling was not approved, including the feeling that ABC was ahead of other news organizations on the story. NBC News President Lawrence K. Grossman, who had proposed the idea, contends that he normally opposes pools on the grounds that competition among the media is likely to insure better service to the public.

Another possibility for change involves government officials as much as media representatives. The target is the "staging" and management of news. Lloyd Cutler has called for exposure of the "tacit conspiracy of silence" about the staging of television news, the political press conferences and public addresses, calling the practice "a fraud." He echoes Boorstin's earlier polemic, *The Image*, in which he refers to such staged events as pseudo-events. Although events are arguably real, whether staged or not, it is the staged events which allow more leeway for policymakers to deceive the public.

Redefining World News

Some media professionals and scholars contend that what is needed is a more radical redefinition of international news as well as basic structural reform in the existing system. Sociologist Herbert J. Gans, in his 1979 book *Deciding What's News*, argued for an alternative conception of news, which he labeled "multiperspectival news." However, Gans' perspective was heavily domestic. If adapted to the problem of world affairs coverage, his proposals and those of others could result in an increase in the quantity as well as the quality of information conveyed by television. Such change could occur if the national networks both expanded their news time and concentrated proportionately more on international affairs. The 40 to 50 percent of airtime devoted to international news on national network television could easily increase to 80 or 90 percent, leaving local and regional coverage to local stations.

A new conception of international news would provide more of a bottom-up view as opposed to a top-down approach. This would require more attention to nonelite nations, organizations and individuals, and relatively less attention to elites. More international news would, by definition, mean more consistent coverage from Africa, large parts of Asia and Latin America. Such coverage could help greatly to broaden public discussion of the U.S. foreign policy agenda. It might also help dispel the sense of sudden surprise that so often accompanies news of U.S. relations with the developing nations of the regions. The revolution in Iran and ensuing hostage crisis was one example. The "sudden" official realization that U.S. policy was on the wrong side in the 1986 revolution in the Philippines was another. The list of nations which are highly important to the United States in policy terms but receive consistently scant attention on television news is longer than one might expect and includes Mexico, Brazil, India and the Republic of Korea.

While commercial pressures are pushing the networks toward

collaborative arrangements with television news organizations in other parts of the world, there is no empirical evidence as yet to document change in established patterns of news coverage.

A new conception of news would also dictate greater attention to long-term processes than to events. In 1966, *New York Times* columnist James Reston called for a new definition of news, "with more attention to the causes rather than merely the effects of international strife." *Many Voices, One World*, the 1980 report of the International Commission for the Study of Communication Problems, made the same point. The report noted that "hunger is a process while a hunger strike is an event; a flood is an event, a struggle to control floods is a process." The evidence to date suggests that commercial television, with its competitive appetite for the visually dramatic, has only exacerbated the problem created by focusing too heavily on events versus processes.

One problem with proposals for radical redefinition of televised international news is the dilemma posed for television journalists. Does their loyalty belong first to their country as U.S. citizens, requiring them to be circumspect in reporting events, processes and views from other nations? Or do they have a higher obligation to promote a free, diverse flow of visual news that includes a multitude of different perspectives? The dilemma is real.

A second problem with proposals for radical redefinition of international affairs coverage by television is that they imply a need for basic structural reforms. An example of such structural reform in the print media is Inter Press Service (IPS), a Third World news agency dedicated to providing coverage of the needs of people in developing nations and efforts to satisfy them, signs of potential movement toward self-reliant development, and facts related to efforts to transform socioeconomic structures.

Although questions of gradual reforms versus more radical change in international news coverage by television may at times appear intractable, they are likely to become ever more important matters of public policy. One reason is the rapid pace of change in the technology for satellite gathering and distribution of television news. Another is the inherently international character of key technologies, which will obligate U.S. television news organizations to operate within certain agreements or limitations shaped by other nations. The press has historically played an important role in foreign policy, but television represents a quantum leap in the media's impact. Television's future performance and the delineation of its responsibilities are inseparable from the challenge of formulating and implementing sensible U.S. policies toward all nations and regions of the world. In that light, the issues and the specific case examples raised here may be viewed as a prologue to global television in the 21st century.

Talking It Over
A Note for Students and Discussion Groups

This issue of the HEADLINE SERIES, like its predecessors, is published for every serious reader, specialized or not, who takes an interest in the subject. Many of our readers will be in classrooms, seminars or community discussion groups. Particularly with them in mind, we present below some discussion questions—suggested as a starting point only—and references for further reading.

Discussion Questions

The Reagan Administration began with the release by Iran of the U.S. hostages and is ending with the Iran-contra affair. How important would these events have been without television coverage? How large a role did television coverage of the Iran hostage crisis play in Jimmy Carter's defeat in the 1980 presidential election?

Why do you think television covers some countries and regions more than others? How does this affect the public's knowledge of, and opinions on, foreign policy issues? How will technology affect the global impact of television news?

Do you think that print journalism or television has more influence on the general public? decisionmakers? opinion leaders?

What is the relationship between the media and foreign-policy makers? Is the relationship an adversarial one? To what extent do policymakers set the television news agenda? To what extent does television news determine the policymakers' agenda?

Television reaches a larger audience than print journalism and the visual nature of TV news reports makes them more accessible, but because of budgetary and other constraints, television coverage of world events tends to be brief and selective. Does TV coverage have a positive or negative effect on popular participation in U.S. foreign policy?

Do you think network newscasts, given their 22-minute time limit, should cover fewer stories in depth, or is it more important to cover more subjects in less detail?

What new roles do you see for television in relation to foreign policy during the next decade?

READING LIST

Adams, William C., ed., *Television Coverage of International Affairs*. Norwood, N.J., Ablex, 1981. Contains an introductory overview chapter and 12 studies of how U.S. television covers international affairs. Includes such diverse topics as coverage of the Third World, presidential diplomacy, the 1980 Olympic boycott, terrorism, war in Southeast Asia, and the question of what information gets across to audiences.

———, ed., *Television Coverage of the Middle East*. Norwood, N.J., Ablex, 1981. A series of original analyses of how the Middle East is depicted on U.S. television news. Includes studies of how leading American journalists view the U.S. relationship with Israel, Anwar al-Sadat's visit to Jerusalem, the Soviet invasion of Afghanistan, and the Iran hostage crisis.

Almond, Gabriel, *The American People and Foreign Policy*, 2nd ed. Westport, Conn., Greenwood Press, 1977. Classic study of public opinion.

Batscha, Robert M., *Foreign Affairs News and the Broadcast Journalist*. New York, Praeger, 1975. A study based on interviews and informal discussions with network television correspondents and producers. A significant contribution because it is the most recent study using such methodology to focus exclusively on international affairs coverage.

Cutler, Lloyd N., "Foreign Policy on Deadline." *Foreign Policy*, Fall 1984. An influential and widely cited article on television's new role in foreign policy, based partly on Cutler's experience in the Carter White House during the Iran hostage crisis.

Epstein, Edward J., *News From Nowhere*. New York, Vintage Books, 1973. The first thorough study of how the three major commercial news organizations operate, based on extensive interviews and observation. Highly readable, it remains a landmark.

Golding, Peter, and Elliott, Philip, *Making the News*. New York, Longman, 1979. A comparative study of television news broadcasting in Sweden, Ireland and Nigeria.

Larson, James F., "Television and U.S. Foreign Policy: The Case of the Iran Hostage Crisis." *Journal of Communication*, Autumn 1986. Uses television coverage of Iran from the early 1970s through the 444-day hostage crisis as a basis for evaluating a series of propositions about the structural relationship of television news and foreign policy.

———, *Television's Window on the World: International Affairs Coverage on the U.S. Networks*. Norwood, N.J., Ablex, 1984. Rigorously quantifies the amount and nature of network television attention to nations and regions of the world from 1971 to 1982. It compares coverage of developed, developing and socialist-bloc nations and examines the influence of satellite technology and the distribution of network bureaus and print media correspondents on patterns of coverage.

Mosettig, Michael, and Griggs, Henry, Jr., "TV At the Front." *Foreign Policy*, Spring 1980. A good, inside look at how satellite technology, competitive pressures and current journalistic practices affect television's international affairs coverage. Written while one of the authors was foreign news producer at NBC television.

O'Neill, Michael J., *Terrorist Spectaculars: Should TV Coverage Be Curbed?* A Twentieth Century Fund Paper. New York, Priority Press Publications, 1986. A provocative monograph by a veteran print journalist, addressing a range of questions about television and terrorism with many current examples. Includes treatment of why television is so different from prior media and suggestions for improving the current situation, including a call for "preventive journalism."

Paletz, David L., and Entman, Robert M., *Media Power Politics*. New York, The Free Press, 1981. Focuses on the relationship between news media and political power in America, with considerable attention to television and one chapter dedicated exclusively to the political impact of media coverage of foreign news.